THE SUCCESS SECRETS TO RETAIL INDUSTRY

GO GREEN OR GET OUT

THE SUCCESS SECRETS TO RETAIL INDUSTRY

GO GREEN OR GET OUT

ANAND BAJORIA

Worldwide Published by
Pendown Press

PENDOWN PRESS

An ISO 9001 & ISO 14001 Certified Co.,

Regd. Office: 2525/193, 1st Floor, Onkar Nagar-A,
Tri Nagar, Delhi-110035

Ph.: 09350849407, 09312235086

E-mail: info@pendownpress.com

Branch Office: 1A/2A, 20, Hari Sadan, Ansari Road,
Daryaganj, New Delhi-110002

Ph.: 011-45794768

Website: PendownPress.com

First Edition: 2021

Price: ₹259/-

ISBN: 978-93-91544-12-6

Layout and Cover Designed by Pendown Graphics Team

Printed and Bound in India by Thomson Press India Ltd.

CONTENTS

INTRODUCTION TO A NATURALLY GREEN LIFE

Dear Reader,

Thank you for choosing this book. The moment you have picked up this book, you have taken the first step on the journey to going Green. This book is your affirmation of a 360-degree change in how you live and how you do Business.

It is my intention that by implementing the simple, practical, yet profound changes I share in this book, you will be able to impact not just your lifestyle and the way you conduct your Business. You will also be able to have a significant positive, eco-friendly impact on the planet as a whole.

So Congratulations on becoming a Climate Change Warrior while simultaneously enhancing profits!

This book gives insight into the demands, expectations, and underlying decision-making reasons for the new age millennial shoppers and the informed, eco-conscious shoppers of today.

The buying behaviour of today's shopper is not just restricted to or driven by cost/competitive pricing/lower pricing. Instead, they focus on: where they are shopping and what they are buying. They are interested in knowing whether the establishment they are buying from cares enough for the environment or not.

The old way of making buying decisions has shifted entirely. The old guard has given way to the new.

Shoppers are becoming increasingly eco-conscious, responsible, and well informed on sustainable issues.

This book will benefit anyone and everyone who picks it up and begins to live it because I share simple tools and techniques that will help every person effortlessly shift to a more sustainable lifestyle both at home and work.

However, if you are in the Homeware or Food Retail Business or a Restaurateur, you cannot afford to miss this book.

In this book, I share step-by-step tools and techniques to enhancing your profitability. By going Green and Sustainable, you will be able to increase profits by leaps and bounds through tapping into the vast potential New-Age Market and attracting and retaining the New-Age-Consumer.

Welcome to the world of Huge Profitability through Easy Sustainability!

As an experienced entrepreneur and entrepreneurial adviser for over twenty-five years, I have guided and advised entrepreneurs and various companies across South Asia and the Middle East in gaining international competitiveness, manufacturing excellence, and enhanced profitability using sustainable products & solutions.

Heading SKICORP – A futuristic group of businesses that empowers entrepreneurs, businesses, and manufacturers in global industries to have system & process-driven efficient production to create a better tomorrow; I consider it my mission to reach out to as many businesses and individuals as I can through this book and guide them to a better lifestyle and better business practices through sustainability.

With the experience of nearly three decades in multiple businesses, we bring together the vision and knowledge to go beyond the expected and find the best possible solutions for our stakeholders. We are known for converting unique ideas into successful businesses that solve our existing and potential customers' challenges and help the world move forward.

I can assure you that I actually practice what I am preaching. I have personally spearheaded and successfully introduced a range of eco-friendly/green – products under the brand name NATURALLYOURS.

These NaturallYours products are being retailed in major gourmet food stores and lifestyle stores and are being used in leading hotels, restaurants, cafes in India and outside India.

I have designed and written this book in such a manner that it will help you and your Business go Green with minimum effort and least disruption. Going Green is something no business will be able to avoid sooner than later as the future is Green. This book allows you to be a part of the pioneering group of Businesses that will not only be socially and environmentally responsible but will ride the Green wave to rake in the Gold of profitability by jumping on to the Green Wagon right now.

The time is now! Go Green or Go out!

NaturallYours,

Your Partner in Sustainability

Anand Bajoria

ACKNOWLEDGEMENT

This book would not have been possible without the unconditional support of my Family Members, Close Friends and the entire SKICORP Team. I would also like to express sincere gratitude to my Mentors and Guides Ms. Laura Vierucci, Mr. R.K Jaggi, Mr. Akshar Yadav and the late Mr. Jai Karmaker for their unstinting guidance, support and motivation.

Finally, I want to thank the entire Pendown Press team headed by Mr. Dinesh Verma for their constant support at every juncture of this project.

Chapter 1

UNDERSTANDING ECO-FRIENDLINESS

What does it mean to be Eco-Friendly?

"Eco-friendly" is a description that can be applied to many different products, including promotional giveaways, packaging, packing materials, and more. It's a term that means something is good for our natural environment. But what makes a product eco-friendly? Who regulates the use of that label? And how do you know if the promotional product that you love is 100% eco-friendly?

What makes an Environmentally Friendly Product?

If you search Google for "what are eco-friendly products," you'll get a large number of articles attempting to answer that question. The truth is that terms like eco-friendly and environmentally friendly are broad terms. Beyond saying that an item is nice for nature, they don't have standard definitions.

But if you read those articles, you'll notice some shared ideas. Basically, there are a few factors that manufacturers and sellers use to say a product is good for the environment.

The materials it contains

Eco-friendly products usually contain material that's been recycled, material that's easily recycled, or material gathered from a natural source, like bamboo, which is easy to replace and minimally damaging to harvest. Environmentally friendly products avoid toxic chemicals known to cause harm.

The way it's produced

An environmentally friendly product can be made in a facility powered by solar power, for example, or in a building designed to use the least amount of water possible.

The manner it's used

Products might encourage environmentally conscious behaviours in consumers. Reusable water bottles, for example, help people avoid buying one-use plastic water bottles, which can clog landfills if not recycled.

When we talk about a promotional product that's 100% eco-friendly, we're most often describing it in terms of the materials it contains. Why? Because it's the easiest to measure. Manufacturers know if their products contain 100% post-consumer recycled material, meaning it contains materials people actually used instead of pre-consumer material from the factory floor.

> Eco-friendly products promote green living that helps conserve energy and prevent air, water, and noise pollution. They prove to be a boon for the environment and also prevent human health from deteriorating.

Chapter 2

GO GREEN OR GO OUT

Why does my Business need to be Eco-Friendly?

With the planet on the verge of a disaster and natural resources on the brink of exhaustion, **Green today is not just the new normal but the only way to go!**

Climate change scares; disastrous incidents like the Amazon fires, oil slicks, excessive consumerism leading to the generation of non-recyclable waste has made the world stop and think.

It has raised our social and environmental conscience and brought about a massive global change in the mentality of consumers.

Consumers today are seeking and demanding natural products and social responsibility!

A green business makes customers feel that it is a trustworthy business!

Eco-friendly products are trending worldwide.

As the increased environmental impacts of the traditional businesses bring a rise in sustainability issues locally and globally, companies are working to develop and market eco-friendly retail products to promote sustainable, eco-friendly consumption patterns.

It is not enough to be competitive with your pricing, quality, and service to succeed. In today's times, it is necessary to differentiate yourself in a saturated market. A great way to differentiate your Business is to be sustainable and green as this is the future. In the future, all businesses will have to be green.

What makes the New-Age Customer happy?

Before buying, a customer considers many factors, and often those are personal preferences. Global awareness of ecological and environmental issues has created a huge shift in the marketplace. The new-age customer is now leaning towards buying sustainable, green, and organic products. They are actively seeking out retailers and manufacturers who are green and environment friendly.

A survey by the reputable agency Nielsen found a massive 66% of consumers out of the considerable sample size of 30,000 consumers worldwide were willing to pay more for products from sustainable sources. The same survey also showed that this percentage rose even higher to 77% when only millenials were surveyed.

This is so much so that according to the latest research by the Global Web Index,57% of consumers would choose sustainable brands even if they were more expensive, and 61% of users were willing to choose a different brand if they discovered that their current brand wasn't eco-friendly.

New-age consumers, more so the younger population, want brands whose values are aligned with theirs. They're insisting on socially conscious mission statements and processes. Their environmental consciousness drives them to consume eco-friendly products and services more.

Will going Green restrict my Business?

NO!!!

Going green doesn't necessarily mean that you will be restricted to selling nothing but products made with organic material.

Even customers understand this approach isn't realistic for many businesses; however, even having a few environmentally conscious products in your range of stock conveys to them your commitment to eco-friendliness. Also, you can incorporate many green practices into your business process without totally altering your existing setup.

In the following chapters, we will look at simple, practical steps to go green and thrive.

How will going green affect my customers?

- **Tap Into The Millennial Market:** Millennials are a massive chunk of the marketplace globally. According to estimation, they spend nearly 600 Billion $ every year, a number expected to grow to $1.4 trillion in the coming years. If you want a market share of this enormous potential, the only way is to go green. Prime examples of this phenomenon are brands like Whole Foods and Tesla, which have cashed on their Business's social and environmental impact.

  A survey by the Shelton Group found that 70% of millenials say a company's environmental focus impacts their purchasing decisions. Though eco-friendly products may be higher priced, millenials consider them as a long-term investment. For example, though priced higher, an LED bulb will last longer and save money on their electricity bill.

- **Enhanced Customer Loyalty:** Eco-friendly products are an easy way to gain consumer trust. As discussed earlier, an eco-friendly business inspires more trust in customers, leading to more engagement with them. A deeper bond with your customers translates into enhanced customer loyalty.
- **Encourage Repeat Purchases:** Increased customer loyalty, in turn, leads to a high level of repeat purchases and inspires word of mouth marketing, resulting in increased Business.

When customers trust you on one product and are loyal to you, they'll be open to buying your other products as well.

Thus it is clear that the deteriorating state of the environment and the increasing environmental consciousness of consumers globally have impelled environmental consciousness within businesses. In the next chapter, we will work on learning to make our business environment-friendly with ease.

You can begin right now and capture the interest of environmentally concerned consumers because there will only be environmentally aligned customers in the future.

All businesses will either have to Go Green or Get Out!

Chapter 3

GOING GREEN WITH EASE

So, How Do I Go Green?

As already established earlier, eco-friendly business measures are essential to save the planet and enhance business profitability as new-age customers are demanding eco-friendly products and organizations.

As promised earlier, you do not have to disrupt your entire operations to go green. You can do so easily by incorporating the following "Pro-Tips" that are simple and practical.

Reduce Paper Usage

Change your printing habits as a business. Only print what you absolutely must. Use virtual storage like cloud, and Google drives, etc., instead of physical files. You can also shift to using 100% PCW (Post-Consumer Waste) paper instead of virgin wood pulp paper.

Use Energy Efficient Lights And Appliances

There are many ways to lower electrical usage without impacting operations. Use CFL and LED lights which use much less energy and last up to 25 years. Use Energy Efficiency Certified equipment such as air-conditioning, freezers, heaters, etc. Use power-saving modes on your PCs etc. Saving energy means saving money. Try using solar power where possible.

Switch to sustainable packaging alternatives

Irrespective of whether you are a Brick & Mortar or an E-commerce presence,the packaging is an inevitable part. You can start making more environmentally conscious packaging decisions by sourcing green packaging material incorporating the '3 Rs' – reduce, reuse, recycle! Packaging is also where you can tell your customer about being Green.

Recycle, Upcycle, And Manage E-Waste

Set up recycling bins as much as possible and tie up with agencies who manage e-waste instead of disposing it off indiscriminately.

Donate

Don't just dump that equipment or assets that are no longer useful to you but are still functional or semi-functional; instead, donate them to NGOs where they can be used by others who need them. This could even be a part of your CSR (Corporate Social Responsibility) initiative.

Revamp Your Office Kitchen/Pantry/Cafeteria

Almost all offices are big on bottled water and Styrofoam coffee cups. These single-use items, however, spell disaster for the planet. Try shifting to reusable glasses and mugs instead. If you have to use disposable items, make sure they are biodegradable.

Go Green When Sourcing

Source the materials that you need for your Business from green organic suppliers. These can even be small things like biodegradable cleaning products to green office supplies like refillable pens and staple-free staplers.

Volunteer For Green Activities

Volunteer for green activities that will help create green initiatives in your community. You can partner with various NGOs who work in ecologically conscious domains.

Enhance Savings The Eco-Friendly Way!

These simple practices of energy conservation, recycling, use of water-saving devices, energy-efficient equipment, solar power, and reduced waste, etc., will not only help you position yourself as a green business and attract more customers but will enhance profits by reducing costs.

> One of the best ways to be a Green Business is to offer one or more Green products in your mix.

Chapter 4

GO GREEN IN STYLE

Are Sustainable Products low on style and aesthetics?

ABSOLUTELY NOT!!!

That is a complete myth!

Consumers and Business owners often have certain patterns of negative associations with sustainable product options. They view them as being less aesthetically pleasing and low on style quotient.

That, however, is a complete myth with numerous sustainable brands in fashion, home ware, and accessories offering options that are trendy, stylish, and comfortable while being Green and Sustainable.

Prime examples of Fashion brands in this category that are sizzling, sexy yet sustainable are:

H & M Conscious

Using materials like organic cotton and recycled polyester, and more sustainable production methods, the company hopes to reduce its environmental footprint without compromising fashion and style.

Levi's

Though Denim requires massive amounts of water to create one pair of jeans, Levi's new collection, water <Less, uses

up to 96% less water. There is no compromise on the style quotient and trendiness, though. In addition, Levi's is committed to sustainability through the entire design and manufacturing process and is trying to move toward 100% sustainably sourced cotton and recycling old jeans into home insulation.

Other than these two prime examples, there are numerous stylishly sustainable fashion brands like Rothys, Reformation, Eileen Fisher, etc.

Examples of Stylish and sustainable Homeware brands:

Weaver Green

Weaver Green is a unique, sustainable initiative; it produces some of the most beautiful hand-loomed rugs, blankets, footstools, cushions, and bags made of 100 percent recycled plastic bottles without compromising its style, feel, or value.

MAiK

MAiK's is a trendy brand that produces timeless contemporary designs made with materials that have been sourced responsibly; they have also developed special plastic-free packaging, which has been carefully developed and sourced to ensure all elements are biodegradable and recyclable. All this without any compromise on style or aesthetics,

Other than these two prime examples, there are numerous stylishly sustainable fashion brands like Koala, One Nine Eight Five, and Buffy,etc.

Indian brands are not lagging on the sustainability front either; many of them such as Mix Mitti, Maati By Neha, Liva, The B-Label, Oorja, The Retyrement Plan, Mishcat, Baro, Differniture and NaturallYours, etc. have broken barriers and created beautiful fashion and lifestyle products that are sustainable and stylish.

Their products are something that everyone wants to own, not simply because they are green eco-friendly products but because they are incredibly stylish while being Green.

> Sustainability and style are not mutually exclusive! Choose from a range of products that are as stylish as they are functional.

Chapter 5

GREEN IS THE NEW GOLD

Swapping to a green lifestyle doesn't have to be a daunting project. For the homemaker, it is easy to step into sustainability by beginning to use kitchenware, storage ware, and environmentally safe décor items.

By shifting to more environmentally safe products, we reduce pollution and contamination of natural resources such as the air, water, and soil, thereby contributing to the planet's safety.

The retail industry is currently seeing rapid growth in the popularity of eco-friendly shopping and the demand for sustainable wares. Retailers can build trust, enhance customer loyalty, and increase profits by offering green products in your mix. The same goes for Gourmet Food Stores and Restaurants as they can start the shift to sustainability by using sustainable kitchenware and tableware.

These 'wow factor' wares are easy to introduce into your life and Business and are sure to boost your mood, decorate your home and lift your spirits along with your style quotient.

Choose environmentally friendly products; it's simple to do.

Through the following "PRO-TIPS," let me show you

four easy ways to go green at home, work, or in your Business… it is as easy as 1, 2, 3, 4...

Tip # 1: Green it up with a Slice of Pizza!

A Pizza is perhaps the first choice of food for youngsters in today's times. No party, outing, or cosy get-together is complete without it. Significantly these youngsters are the ones who are most passionate about saving the environment and going green.

A great way to shift to sustainability is to go green with the packaging and serving of Pizzas and other millennial-friendly and party-friendly foods.

Unique, sustainable Pizza trays and serving dishes for other kinds of foods are a great way to go sustainable in your home, food business, or offering them up as a green product in your retail store/chain.

Platter it out in style while you do your bit to save the planet.

Tip # 2: Going Baskets over Sustainability!

Baskets are genuinely worth going baskets over. They are perhaps the most versatile and multi-usage products ever. Also, baskets have traditionally always been made out of natural and eco-friendly materials such as jute, wicker, bamboo, hemp, palm and coconut leaves, etc.

Baskets come in all shapes and sizes, and they can be used for serving, storing, carrying, and as pure décor items even.

Serving breads and other suitable dishes in sustainable baskets at home and restaurants is a great and easy way to go green.

Sustainable Baskets are great for storing stationery items, knick-knacks, books, and even laundry storage at home and work. Retailers don't miss offering baskets as an opportunity to tap into a substantial environment-conscious clientele.

Baskets are great for arranging Fruits and Flowers too.

And yes, Baskets are mobile too; use them to carry stuff around, picnics, or even office.

Baskets make excellent Home Décor pieces too!

And… don't forget Baskets make for great Gift Hampers too…

Tip # 3: Saving The Planet One Bowl at a time!

Bowls are essential parts of our lives; throughout our day, no matter where we are or whether we are alone or in company, we will definitely end up using a bowl at one time or another.

It's almost like bowls hold our entire world; they hold food that nourishes us, they hold stuff that satisfies our sweet or savory cravings, they are our eternal companions at munch time, and they even help us, welcome friends and family with joy and warmth as we offer them, love, through snacks and savories laid out in bowls.

So a small shift in the kind of bowls we choose translates into a significant shift in our lifestyle.

This single choice of shifting to a sustainable bowl can truly be a golden choice that impacts us and the planet positively. Also, for retailers and food businesses, this is an act of social responsibility that will also enhance profitability.

Bowls, again like baskets, are immensely versatile and can be used in a variety of ways:

Fortify and nourish yourselves with fruits and salads in an eco-friendly bowl, and you can nurture the planet too…

Layout some love for the planet as you welcome guests into your home and heart, choose green bowls, make a difference…

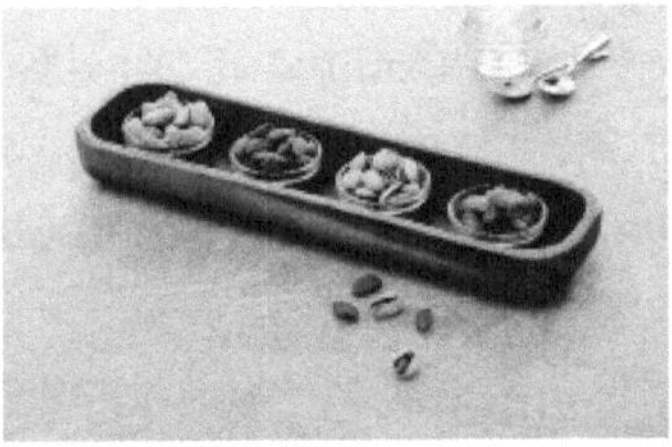

Munch consciously and make movie time that much better; a small choice makes a big impact. Just as you choose healthy snacks, choose a bowl that is healthy for the planet too…

Spice it up or sweeten your life because either way,you deserve to be rewarded for your conscious choice of eco-friendly bowls…

Tip # 4: Chop out the Toxicity!

Every household needs to chop up fruits, veggies, cheeses, etc., and most households use a chopping board to facilitate this. A small and easy way to shift into a green lifestyle is to bid goodbye to plastic chopping boards consciously. These are toxic and non-biodegradable, thus harming your health and that of the environment.

Choose a sustainable yet stylish wooden chopping board and chop up the toxicity forever.

There is a huge variety of sturdy, stylish, and sustainable Chopping Boards available in the market to choose from…

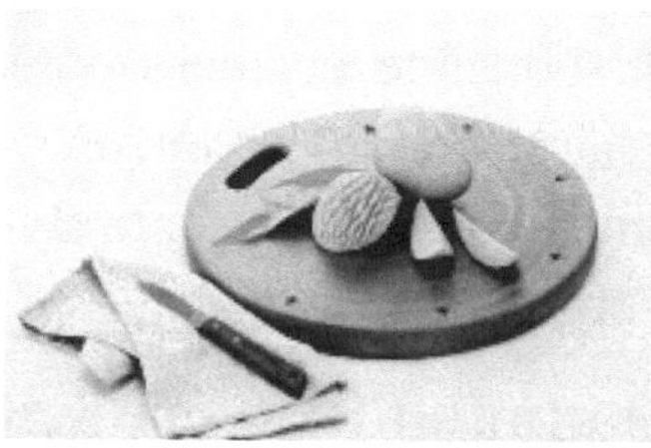

Thus it is not difficult to take that first step on your journey to going green, the important thing is to make that conscious choice, and these simple tips will make it really easy for you.

Chapter 6

BE SUSTAINABLE & PROFITABLE; MAKE EVERY DAY EARTH DAY!

As discussed earlier in chapter 2, in view of the stressful climate change situation and the overall ecological degeneration of the planet, consumers no longer have the patience for brands that are not focused on ethical and environmentally conscious business practices. Even governments around the world are recognizing the importance of responsible business practices that, at the very least, do not harm the environment. There is tremendous pressure on businesses to create entirely sustainable models with a low to zero carbon footprint.

Sustainability is critical

Consumers see an emotional connection; Sustainability impacts consumers' purchase preferences and makes them happy.

The retail industry is currently witnessing massive and rapid growth in the popularity of eco-friendly shopping and the demand for sustainable fashion, lifestyle, and home products.

Any brand that ignores meaningful sustainability is looking at a future that will be shunned by the extremely aware Millennials and GenZs.

> Consumers are increasingly demanding natural products and social responsibility.

There is no denying the facts:

- Nearly 80% of consumers want to make a difference in saving the planet for future generations.
- 77% are concerned about the humane and fair treatment of workers.
- 72% are personally concerned about their environmental footprint.
- 66% choose to purchase products or services based on their "environmental friendliness."

Retailers and restauranteurs have a crucial role to play here, as they can influence lifestyles with great ease. They have a moral and social responsibility to create awareness by using these kinds of products and offering them to customers who are looking to make eco-friendly lifestyle changes.

Believe me; you will be ably rewarded for your efforts because Green is the new Gold. It is the only way to tap into the new-age customer, retain them and remain profitable.

> Increased demand for Eco-friendly products means more profitability if you promote them. It also makes you more Socially Responsible. There is no reason you cannot be Sustainable and Profitable! Going Green is no longer a choice; it is your only option!

Notes:

Notes:

Notes: